Haunt Me

José Enrique Medina

Rattle | Studio City, California | 2025

Haunt Me
Copyright © 2025 by José Enrique Medina

All rights reserved

Layout and design by Timothy Green

Cover art by Abraham Gomez
"Wind Chimes," 2025

ISBN: 978-1-931307-62-8

First edition

Rattle Foundation
12411 Ventura Blvd
Studio City, CA 91604
www.rattle.com

The Rattle Foundation is an independent 501(c)3 nonprofit, whose mission is to promote the practice of poetry, and which is not affiliated with any other organization. All poems are works of the imagination. While the perceptions and insights are based on the author's experience, no reference to any real person is intended or should be inferred.

Contents

Niños de la Tierra	7
Three Ghosts	8
The Dead Are Bored Back to Life	10
Tío Arturo's Manifesto	11
I Carve Figures of My Dead	12
Like Rare Pokémon Cards, We Go Through Life Collecting the Dead	13
Wake Up	15
The Cold of Serious Intent	16
Día de los Muertos Baking Contest	18
The Chair I Pull Out	19
Haunt Me	20
When Mother Doesn't Visit Me, I Worry	21
We Interrupt This Book to Bring You an Important Message	22
A Fistful of Cursed Desert	24
I Hear a Ferryboat's Horn Mooing	26
Broken Seashells	27
My Mother's Buried in the Largest Cemetery in North America	29
Even Without a Body	31
Last Call	32
Daily Practices	34
Acknowledgments	37
Encore! Encore! Encore!	39

Haunt Me

for Elizabeth Vega

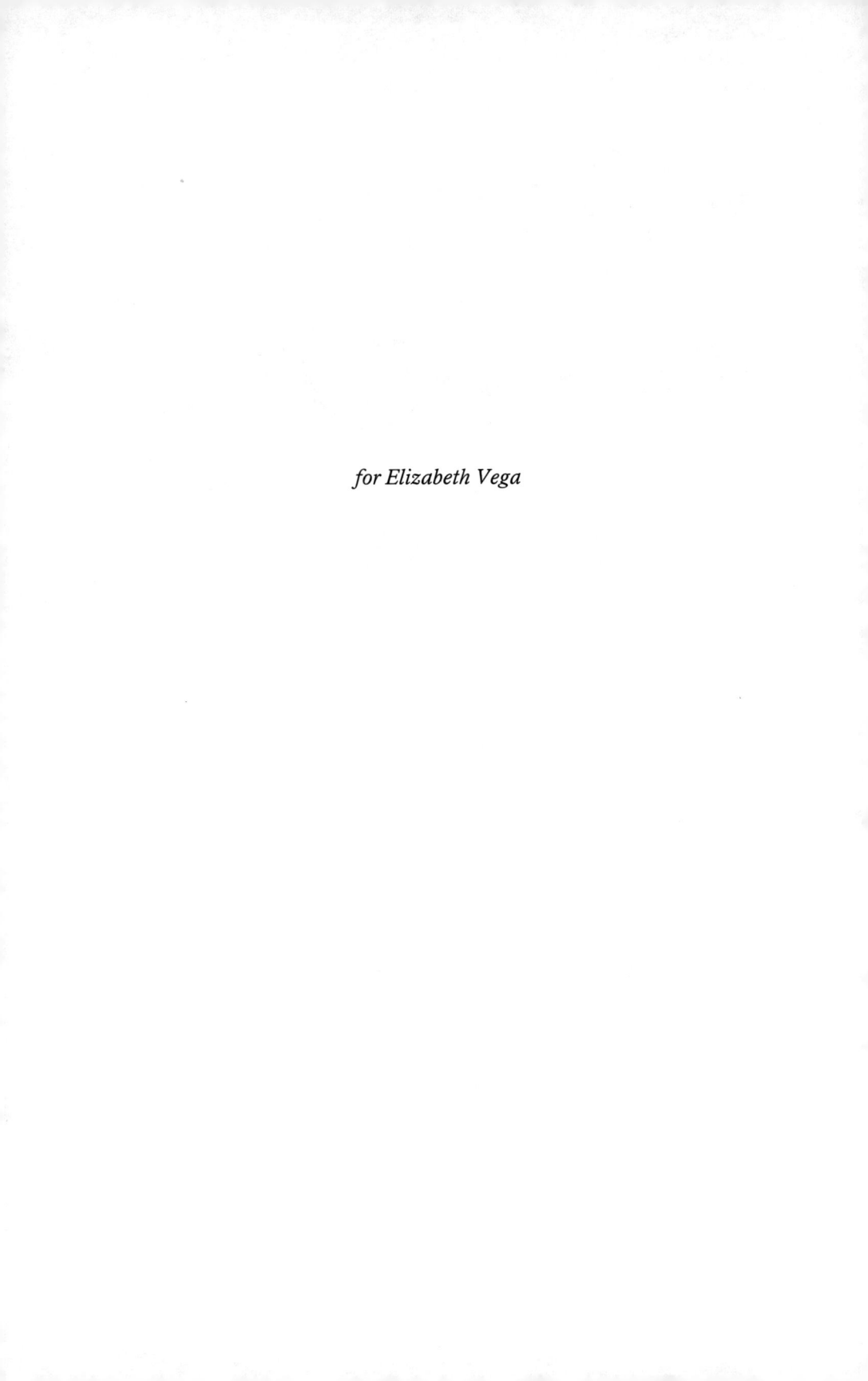

Niños de la Tierra

I grew up believing there were children under the earth. "When it rains, they come out," Abuela said, wrapped tight in the exoskeleton of her rebozo. "One sting, and you're dead." After a storm, my little brothers and I guarded the windows with plastic swords, watching mud shine in moonlight. "They're bald like newborns," Abuela whispered with her mothball breath. "They cry like a child." We listened, between wind's pauses, for their wail. If we broke a plate, she frowned, her face wrinkled like caterpillar skin. "They have six legs and little baby fingers at the end of each leg. They kidnap bad kids." We hid, curled in blankets like cocoons. Her face veiled in spidery lace, she slammed her hand against the front door. We huddled together. "Don't go outside. The children of the earth will get you." "What are they?" we asked. "They're Satan's children. Part baby, part tiger." One day, I flipped her the middle finger. "I'm going to grab that little finger and twist it and give it to the earth babies," she snarled. "They'll drag you to hell."

When Abuela died, we found a dead cockroach and pretended it was her. We buried her in the backyard. Then we sprinkled holy water, sealing the grave and trapping her underground.

All that summer, we ran on top of her, laughing in a garden of swollen roses.

Three Ghosts

1.
Abuela doesn't respect international borders—she crosses
El Río Grande, floats into my apartment in East LA.
She died from breast cancer, was buried in Mexico.
She rifles through drawers,
finds gay porn magazines, and says, *Qué gross*.
She scurries off and attends mass three times a day
like she did when she was alive. Tomorrow,
she'll search through my dresser again,
frown at naked men, and mutter, *Qué gross*,
like she has for thirty years. I want to ask,
What are you looking for?
But it's useless to hang words
on ears of shadow.

2.
A pro boxer, Tío Arturo punched Mom's face,
slammed her head against a concrete wall. *No salgas
con hombres*, he said, though she was separated from my father.
She didn't speak to him for decades. Then he got
prostate cancer. Quiet, respectful, she stepped
into the hospital waiting room. Tío's wife
squeezed her hand, *Gracias por venir*.
Weeks later, I walk, dazed, beneath leafless trees,
unable to row the ocean of her forgiveness,
thinking of her blood-sealed eye, thinking
that pity's made my mother crazy.

3.
It's dark, but if you squint you'll see a twisted shape,
a hunchedbacked woman in the tiny garage-converted apartment,
aluminum foil canceling windows. Nonstop,
Tía Tencha scratches her forehead, the spot where the cancer
started. The scab falls, exposing pink meat. It regrows
bigger, and again she tears it off. She mumbles,
Crickets are trying to get me, claws at her scalp, shrinks
from light, refuses to go outside. The crust is scarab-shaped,
grows back wider, fatter. She holds it
in her hand, strokes it, and whispers, *Sleep, chiquito, sleep.*

The Dead Are Bored Back to Life

Tía Tencha, Tío Arturo y Abuela walked for what burned
like a century. Red dust caked under their huaraches.
A road, straight and infinite. The sun—round and enormous—
half-dipped into the horizon like a bloody Eucharist.
Frozen, the red sunset drenched ghosts in pink light.
Tío Arturo said, *I'm tired of on and on. Let's go back.*
They slashed a gash in the red, and stepped into my backyard.

Now, they lounge by my pool, enjoying shade and breeze.
Blue light, rippling off the water, revives them like sap.
I'd like to tell them, *Leave,*
but the desire, always and mysteriously, dies.
Fully clothed, they seem out of place, dangerous,
like thorns on a nopal.
Abuela swats at a fly that isn't there, curses under her breath.
Tía picks at the scab on her forehead,
leaves behind a trail of crusts, my inheritance.
Tío spreads his legs, makes room for his big balls,
invades my space. He closes his eyes,
puts his hands behind his head, and says,
Time for a siesta.

Tío Arturo's Manifesto

An old man has the right
to become a ghost.
An old man, finally, can
retreat to an abandoned beach.

Each morning, the hooves of a mare
score a language into damp sand,
which, loosely translated, asks:
Are you leaving already?
It never writes, thank God,
*Who did you hurt
to deserve vanishing?*

An old man may tuck
black cockatoo feathers in his hair
and call them
his darkest thoughts.

If left alone long enough,
he'll learn to mimic the wind,
blowing through cupped hands,
whistling himself away.

But even a ghost leaves bruises.
Even a vanished man
echoes in bone.

I Carve Figures of My Dead

I chisel a sarcastic curl at the corner of Tía Tencha's lips, then etch a line of despair between her sad eyes. *If I were to draw you*, the doll says, *I'd make your head four times bigger than your body.* Just like when she was alive, I ignore her childlike outbursts. Instead, I blow wood curls out of her face, admire the carved melancholy.

I set the muñeca on the counter and stand. Chingado! Three hours on a plastic milk crate, and all that time, without me knowing, the damn seat was carving its diamond pattern into my flesh. I touch my rear. Pain clamps like metal teeth on both cheeks. Stiff as wood, I can't walk or flex my butt muscles.

How strange—why did I feel nothing while the crate was cutting me? Why did agony strike like a single lightning bolt when I stood?

Foolish nephew, Tía's effigy laughs, *don't you know? Pain is the door that opens onto life—the flash that opens your eyes onto death.*

Like Rare Pokémon Cards,
We Go Through Life Collecting the Dead

Look, let me show you my collection.
It's worth more than my sterling silverware.
This card, folded in half and curling at the edges,
is my first death: Abuela.
No, that's not vinegar you're smelling,
that's her stubbornness, her
Don't-Touch-Me-With-Your-Chusma-
Because-I'm-A-Woman-Of-God stench.

Oh shit! I almost forgot Abuelo's card,
one blind blue eye, one brown eye.
It's so easy to forget the good ones.
I mean, it's so much more fun
badmouthing those who wronged us,
it makes the days spin faster.

This one's worth less—some cousin
who overdosed in Mexico.
I barely knew him. I keep the card,
only because we're blood,
and because I never answered his messages.
Thought he just wanted money.

Ay ay ay, these two, though,
are gem mint: Tía Tencha y Tío Arturo.
They died when I was old enough
to understand death meant
I'd rot like cardboard too.
But let's not talk about that.

[...]

And this, this is my favorite one:
a photo of my mother.
Sorry, I can't show you.
Some things are too special.

Time passes,
and my binder grows, thick with ghosts.

But, enough about me.
Go on. Show me your collection.
Don't be shy.

Wake Up

Here is the night,
I place it in your hands

like a cup.
Drink and remember

having a tongue,
tasting coffee.

*I'm cold,
and it hurts to be in air,*

I think I hear you say.
Let me snore under mud.

I shatter the cup
against your headstone.

Mother,
stir the darkness,

so I can hear
the soft clink of your spoon

against ceramic
again.

The Cold of Serious Intent

I walk along the memory of Tío Arturo,
follow the border of mesquite trees
he planted the summer he arrived
in the USA. Sitting on the cinder-block
bench he built with his own hands,
I feel the cold of serious intent
seep through my jeans.

Tío built this house from cinder and spit.
Now it watches me from every wall.
You're losing time, he says.
Accomplishing nothing—just playing Nintendo 64,
jacking off until your pito swells
like a beet. Cochino. I bolt
from his voice, dive into the dark
of mother's old bedroom, pray
the house keeps its eyes shut. The silence
sighs with the breath of almost presence,
Abuela's chocolate still drifting
from undusted shelves. I touch the hearts
my mother crocheted, stroke pink ribbons.

Why wasn't I born a woman,
instead of this useless man?
Easy to imagine myself female:
my nose fine and upturned like hers,
eyes soft and sagging. In her closet,
I find a dress, once yellow, now quiet with dust.
It smells bitter like sorry.

I press coarse cloth to my chest,
smooth its weight down my body.
In the mirror, my mother's eyes
stop me and ask,

Would you dare put on my dress?

Día de los Muertos Baking Contest

I grab my mom's old Bundt pan, the one she used to bake our birthday cakes, and pour in the batter. Shit, I forgot the sour cherries. Last year, three ghosts—Abuela, Tío Arturo, and Tía Tencha—judged the Día de los Muertos Baking Contest. They tasted my Pan de Muertos and said, *It's pretty good, but it needs something tart.* Should I add the cherries now? No. Abuela always said, *Nothing tastes worse than an afterthought.*

So I keep going, grating fresh coconut at full speed. My mom's favorite fruit. I sprinkle the shreds like white hairs across the surface. They sink slowly, soft gestures of goodbye.

Working against the midnight deadline, I open the oven door, slide the pan in and set the timer for 20 minutes and 19 seconds, the year my mom died. There's nothing left to do but wait. I wipe sweat and flour from my forehead, pour a glass of wine, swirl it, and breathe in the scent. I remember how she showed me to loop cinnamon twists, dust them with cinnamon and piloncillo, pinch the edges like angels' wings.

Her face appears on the curve of the wine glass. *Don't burn the bread,* she says. *Last year you baked it too long.* She says it in that voice of hers—so sweet and annoying at the same time.

I say, *I know, Chepis, I know.*

The Chair I Pull Out

I lower the record-needle. The hoarse voice
of Chavela Vargas starts singing,
Tengo miedo de buscarte y de encontrarte.
I set five plates on the table,
one for me, four for ghosts.
Lighting a candle centerpiece,
I perfume the night with vanilla.
El Niño de Atocha, a child saint,
flickers on the glass, scorched,
as if touched by fire.
The song scrapes its knuckles—
Paloma negra, eres la reja de un penar.
Beside Abuela's plate, I fold the handkerchief
she used to press against the corduroy
of wrinkled lips. On Tencha's napkin
I pinch a mandarin, release her favorite
sting of citrus. In Arturo's glass, I pour
Clamato—*good for la cruda*,
he used to say.
The record rips off the last bandage—
Y arrancarme ya los clavos de mi pena.
Mother is too much to fit in any one thing,
too much hug, too much voice, too much absence.
So I leave her placemat bare,
and pull out her chair.
Once they're all here,
I'll cross myself and say,
Now we can eat.

Haunt Me

Against the greenhouse he built, the soul
of Tío Arturo leans, smelling faintly of brillantina.
Abuela drifts beneath cherry blooms,
thumbing her rosary, whispering prayers.

Mother, where are you?
Even the twins, who were never born, are here,
tossing big-headed mums, each one
a soft grenade of memory.
You died four years ago,
your silence unfolding like petals.

And still
you haven't stepped into my garden
or caressed my amapola blossoms.
What are you waiting for? Haunt me.

Crush lemongrass under your heels,
let me smell you. Ring wind chimes
when there's no breeze, so I'll know.

Or become the breeze itself,
and lift my petals one more time.
Eyes open, ears wide, I wait.

But you never come.
The twins giggle,
brush against my flowers,
and pollinate your absence.

When Mother Doesn't Visit Me, I Worry

What if my mom
isn't where they buried her?
What if somebody stole her cadaver,
and right now is holding up
a liquor store with her jawbone?

*Hand over the cash
or I'll whack you to hell!*

What if they're dismantling her skeleton
and selling the bones
as used car parts at a junkyard?

What if she's being held hostage
in a golden cage,
and force-fed only melon triangles?

What if she eloped,
driving to Las Vegas in a convertible,
Death riding shotgun
(Death who'd make a terrible stepdad)?

What if she hit her head,
lost her key to heaven,
and is wandering the Mojave desert,
unable to find her way home?

We Interrupt This Book to Bring You an Important Message

This just in:
un loco has escaped the Hospital
for the Criminally Insane. He thinks he's a cop
because he's always enforcing the rules of writing.
Once, he refused to shower
because the bathroom sign said "baño" without the tilde.
Correction: Spanish? Please—he barely knows English,
but you get the picture.

Oh—right, picture! Here's his mug shot:
an orphan with ankle-length hair.
When he's sad, which is always,
he droops like a drenched orchid.

He's notorious for doodling puppies
on other people's napkins,
cute, yes,
but with criminal intent.

If you want to avoid him,
go to his mother's grave.
He never visits.
Says his throat might crack like ceramic.
Says her name got stuck in his teeth,
and he's been tonguing it ever since.
Honestly, he should be locked up
for never bringing her flowers.

If you encounter this man,
alone or with a blue finch
that sings to soothe him,
DO NOT engage. He is considered
armed with grief,
and if provoked by the smallest thing,
will recite a long and violoncello-swayed epic
of how he lost his mother
when he was just 50 years old.

We now return to your regularly scheduled heartache.

A Fistful of Cursed Desert

I think often
about returning to a stain on the map of Zacatecas,
where winds whistle between pencas of nopales,
and scarecrows nod their sombreros
like men who've seen too much.
In the shower, crouched and shivering,
I daydream of riding a broken-down bus
to La Villita, that busted-lip pueblo
where my parents were born.
After all, beginnings are dark,
or should be, if you're named Medina,
a name clotted with blood,
sealed in spit and the rot of old wounds.
I was born there, too.
A scorpion nearly took me at one.
That was the year my father peeled off his face
and smiled at my mother with bone.
I won't recount—not with scandal or spite—
how he pounded wicked into her.
The dirt remembers. Bruises grow roots.
What good is roadkill? I'm no vulture
to gnaw tendons, to savor the vinegar of No.
Still, the ghosts call me.
Come back, they say. *Walk the patios*
where your parents braved
dry summers, winters of dust devils.
There must be something sacred,
or cursed, about land wormed with La Llorona,
duendes who snatch children,
sinkholes licking their fingers
after swallowing abuelas whole.
And El Diablo—his hoofprints in the sand,
chicken, horse—erased by morning wind

like omens only the dead can read.
As a toddler, I crawled into the United States,
smuggled a fistful of haunted desert.
Now grown, I carry grains of that sand in my wrinkles.
Beneath my fingernails, the brown dirt grins
and whispers,
Quique—when are you coming home?

I Hear a Ferryboat's Horn Mooing

The smell of cotton candy kicks formaldehyde's
ass, and the clowns laugh, slapping their knees.
A casket doesn't fit in booths crammed
with goldfish bowls. We're at Coney Island,
swallowing hotdogs, dunking the Lady
of Ever-Changing Faces, and screaming
on flame-spitting roller coasters.
If you weren't my mother,
this is the part where I'd throw you
against the strong-man cutout and kiss you.
Love makes fools of borders.
To tease you, I lisp your name three times
and we run laughing into the hall of mirrors
where we stretch and waver like ghosts.
I drag you to the game gallery's grit and glare.
Slow down, mijo, you say. *My heart's weak.*
I pop a balloon and win a life-size giraffe.
The stuffed animal wobbles, giddy as a child.
It can barely stand.
I turn to say, I won for you,
but spinning roses block my view.
You are nowhere, and you've absconded
with the festival's fizz and fun and flash.

Broken Seashells

Since you got sick, I've been turning over
the word *retreat*. It can mean a sergeant barking,
Retreat!, and a bombed-out regiment fleeing—
or a spa weekend for a fabulous gay boy
getting a pedicure at the Ritz.
I love a word that swings both ways—
seven letters that say *Soldier, run for cover*,
or *Girl, this makeover slays*.
But there's a third meaning, quieter:
to withdraw, not from war or into luxury,
but into yourself, because you need the dark.
Enter the snail, hauling its exit
on its back, a soft thing
in a hard shell. I vanish too
when white boys shout *spic*
and flush me from English-only restrooms;
when you drool, tremble,
and doctors look away;
when the world's a chainsaw
and I'm soft-hearted wood;
when seas split open
and I can't straddle both shores.
I brought you to the retreat of this page
to ask you: What if we're born already wounded?
Have you ever felt like a mollusk
with a broken shell? That you can't close
the gap that's unmaking you?
Some days, I carry the rubble
like it's a badge: *Look at me,
I drag my wreckage everywhere.*
Other days, I want to give up,
let the tide take me. But here's the silver lining:

[...]

you're just as fucked,
dragging your broken home,
doubting your sanity,
still crawling.
And even as I hide inside
my busted shell,
I like knowing you're out there
on some dark beach,
safe, dreaming,
your fortress—
just the world's softest pillow.

My Mother's Buried in the Largest Cemetery in North America

Where did I leave her grave?
Dazed, I lean against a tree
to steady the sway. I don't drink,
but I feel drunk with goodbye.
I say, *I'm hungover*, but mean,
Burrrp, who poured this grief so strong?
Sleep starved, I stumble,
can't walk right, like my mother,
crushed under two tons of earth,
mud mixed with what? Patrón?
Don Julio? What was her favorite tequila?
I can't pretend I've never
swallowed oblivion
like a shot poured on a tomb
carved with her name.
Is that her voice?
My mother, is she everybody's mother?
Is there more than one woman in the world?
Do we reel together in shared loss
or die alone, hungover with grief?
I take a step. Trip.
Am I so fucked up that I can't even
find her grave? I clench my fists,
shout, *Ay Jalisco, no te rajes!*
what Mexican drunks scream
when they throw one back.
Yesterday burns going down my throat,
like swallowing her small eyes,
like devouring the past.
Wait. I'm falling.

[...]

Let me grab this branch,
find my footing.
It's so dark.
I swear I left my mother
here,
somewhere,
in this tangle of trees.

Even Without a Body

I curl around you,
a tadpole of caresses,
a touch becoming thought.

You're not only light,
you're a column of warmth,
the hush where language begins.

We drift in yesterday,
no dawn, no dusk,
only the breath before time.

A tide of clocks
lifts us like a wave
and washes us into now.

I reach toward
the future of your face
and say: *I choose you
to be my mother.*

You open,
a murmur blooming,
a lake that says yes,
a gate made of radiance.

I'm a moth-flame,
folding into your soft shimmer,
and for a moment,
they can't tell us apart.

Last Call

When I'm fucked up, really fucked up,
three corpses appear, drinking beer.

Not you cabrones again, I say.
Find another fucking bar. Leave me alone.

Their hands are purple, fingernails splintered
like snapped toothpicks. They smell
like squashed worms, like damp underwear
stuffed behind a radiator.

I grab my drink and start to stagger off,
but ... but ... I haven't talked to anyone in weeks.
And chingue su madre, they don't smell *that* bad.
I've gotten used to my own stench,
vomit on my shirt, bile in my beard.

So I sit.
Tell the bartender, *Give my friends another round.
I'm paying.*

He looks at me like I'm loco. Turns away.

*Abuela. Tío. Tía.
Why do you just sit there,
nodding, silent, glug glug glug?*

I lean closer.
Abuela's earrings catch the light—half-moons
with gold vines curled like cursive.
I smell her lavender talc.

I miss Tío's dumb pranks,

how he'd sneak chile into the Kool-Aid.
I miss Tía's mole, her belly laughs,
how she'd rub Vicks on my chest
when my cough wouldn't quit.

I slump on the stool.
Let the bottle drop.

The three of them
stare at the calendar behind the bar,
a whole month crossed out
with big, black X's.

Daily Practices

Feed the chickens. Clean the bunnies. Weed the raspberries.
Then check your watch, and say, *Chingado, it's already seven.*

Toss the hoe, and lock the barn. Look up:
sky flickering like a red tire fire inside a can of black clouds.

Brush off the warmth of dirt and feathers.
Forget how much you loved the day.
Know this is when the house changes shape.
Let the old door open.

Whistle: *Puuuruuu, puuuruuu.*
When pigeons land, claws scratching your arm,
say, *Ok, papis. Time to sleep.*

Climb into bed. Turn on the TV.
Let the canned laughter convince you you're not alone,
there are still people in the house.

The dead don't count. Ignore Abuela's heels clacking in the hallway.
Fan away Tía Tencha, who returns as the scent of chorizo con huevos.
Close the blinds on Tío Arturo, a figure leaning against the porch post.

Tell yourself: *The departed are nothing—just sounds
scattered through an open window, things you hear, then forget.*

Cross your hands over your chest. Sink into your pillow.
And stay very quiet. Practice being dead, with nothing to do.

Acknowledgments

Gracias to the following journals where versions of these poems first appeared:

San Diego Poetry Annual: "Tío Arturo's Manifesto"
Santa Clara Review: "Día de los Muertos Baking Contest" and "Three Ghosts"
The Burnside Review: "Niños de la Tierra"

Blessings to:

Robert Carr, for putting up with my terrible first drafts for ten years
Elizabeth Vega, friend & supporter since junior high
The Pterodidactyls—Nancy Lynée Woo, Jeanette Kelly, Robin Axworthy, Frank Kearns & Terri Niccum—beautiful poets who pushed me to write this book
Jen Cheng, Poet Laureate of West Hollywood & master of too many damn trades
Mary-Jane Holmes, amazing poet, teacher & friend
Willie Perdomo, former Poet Laureate of New York, mentor & badass homie
The chickens who follow me for food
& the ghosts who haunt me.

Encore! Encore! Encore!

When the dead crawl out of the walls,
I do a strip tease. Show off my big belly
scribbled with hairs, chicken legs,
hands and feet yellow as Bart Simpson.
The departed hound the perfume
of my bare skin. Abuela swoons—
Tío Arturo and Tía Tencha catch her.

But sometimes, during my strut,
I wonder what it means to be loved
only by those whose touch can't leave a mark.

I open the fridge. Cold hardens my nipples,
freezer mist curling around me
like luxurious locks of hair. I cover
my privates like Botticelli's Venus.

My admirers bite their not-fingers,
dying for a chance to be
meat and bone again. I take out
a popsicle, lick it slow. Qué delicious.
They lean in, starved for flavor.
Trapped in paradise, they miss their flesh,
the cruel pleasure of bruise,
the finger-sucking joy of having five senses.

With ghosts for fans, my days are never dull.
Even tossing a popsicle stick has them gasping.
Out of shape, out of work and friendless,
I'm a loser in the eyes of the living,
but a star in the glow of the afterlife,
striking sexy poses
for eyes made eternal by death.

About the Rattle Chapbook Series

The Rattle Chapbook Series publishes and distributes a chapbook to all of *Rattle*'s print subscribers along with each quarterly issue of the magazine. Most selections are made through the annual Rattle Chapbook Prize competition (deadline: January 15th). For more information, and to order other chapbooks from the series, visit our website.

2025	*no matter how it ends a bluebird's song* by Kat Lehmann
	Haunt Me by José Enrique Medina
2024	*Cheap Motels of My Youth* by George Bilgere
	In Which by Denise Duhamel
	Sky Mall by Eric Kocher
2023	*The Fight Journal* by John W. Evans
	At the Car Wash by Arthur Russell
	Plucked by Miracle Thornton
2022	*Imago, Dei* by Elizabeth Johnston Ambrose
	The Morning You Saw a Train of Stars … by CooXooEii Black
	Visiting Her in Queens Is More Enlightening … by Michael Mark
2021	*The Death of a Migrant Worker* by Gil Arzola
	A Plumber's Guide to Light by Jesse Bertron
	I Will Pass Even to Acheron by Amanda Newell
2020	*Adjusting to the Lights* by Tom C. Hunley
	A Juror Must Fold in on Herself by Kathleen McClung
	Falling off the Empire State Building by Jimmy Pappas
2019	*The Last Mastodon* by Christina Olson
	Hansel and Gretel Get the Word on the Street by Al Ortolani
	Did You Know? by Elizabeth S. Wolf
2018	*To Those Who Were Our First Gods* by Nickole Brown
	Tales From the House of Vasquez by Raquel Vasquez Gilliland
	Punishment by Nancy Miller Gomez
	A Bag of Hands by Mather Schneider
2017	*In America* by Diana Goetsch
	The Whetting Stone by Taylor Mali
2016	*3arabi Song* by Zeina Hashem Beck
	Kill the Dogs by Heather Bell
	Ligatures by Denise Miller
	Turn Left Before Morning by April Salzano

www.**Rattle**.com